Copyright © 2021 by Yellow Daisy Publishing

All rights reserved. No part of this book may be used or reproduced in any manner whatsoever without the prior written permission of the author. All inquiries about this book can be sent to the author at AJ.yellowdaisypub@gmail.com

Published in the United States by Yellow Daisy Publishing LLC
ISBN 978-1-953556-03-5

Seesaw Learning, Inc. has granted written permission to the author and Yellow Daisy Publishing to reference Seesaw and the Seesaw app. Seesaw can be accessed at app.seesaw.me and the app is available in most mobile device app stores.

Written permission has been received by the author and Yellow Daisy Publishing to use Mystery Doug. Mystery Doug is owned by Mystery.org and is available at MysteryDoug.com.

Find more books like this or to book an event, visit our website:
www.AJKikumoto.com
www.yellowdaisypub.com

Let's Get Social!

Instagram: @zoeysgreatadventures1   Facebook: Zoey's Great Adventures

Thank you

To Charles Kikumoto for being the best dad ever and helping create an environment for the kids to learn from home.

We love and appreciate your servant heart.

Dedicated to my loving husband Charles who supports all of my activities and projects, including writing and publishing children's books.

This book belongs to:
_____
_____

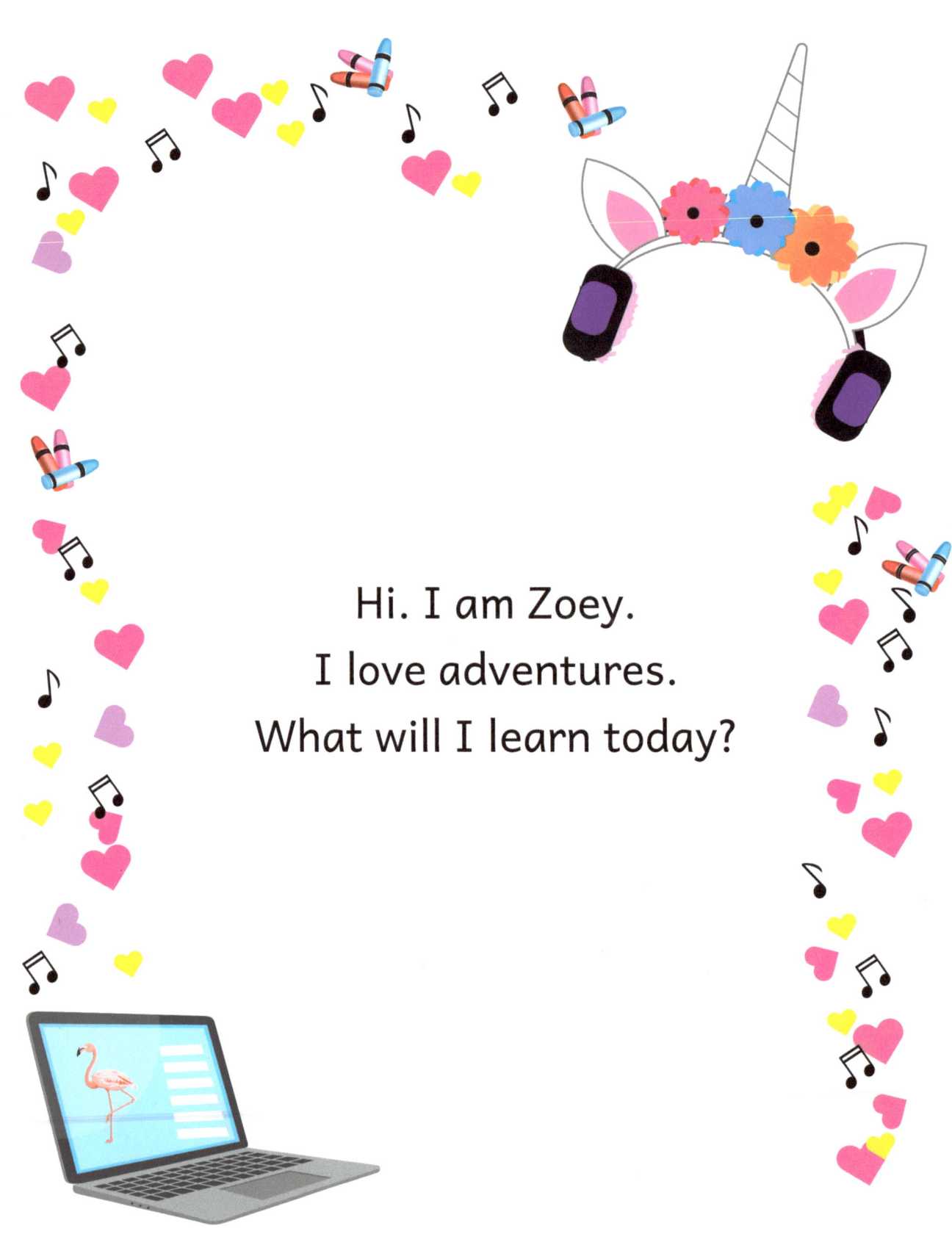

Hi. I am Zoey.
I love adventures.
What will I learn today?

A nasty virus came along and created a world pandemic.
I have to wear a mask to protect myself and others.
My school is not full time anymore.

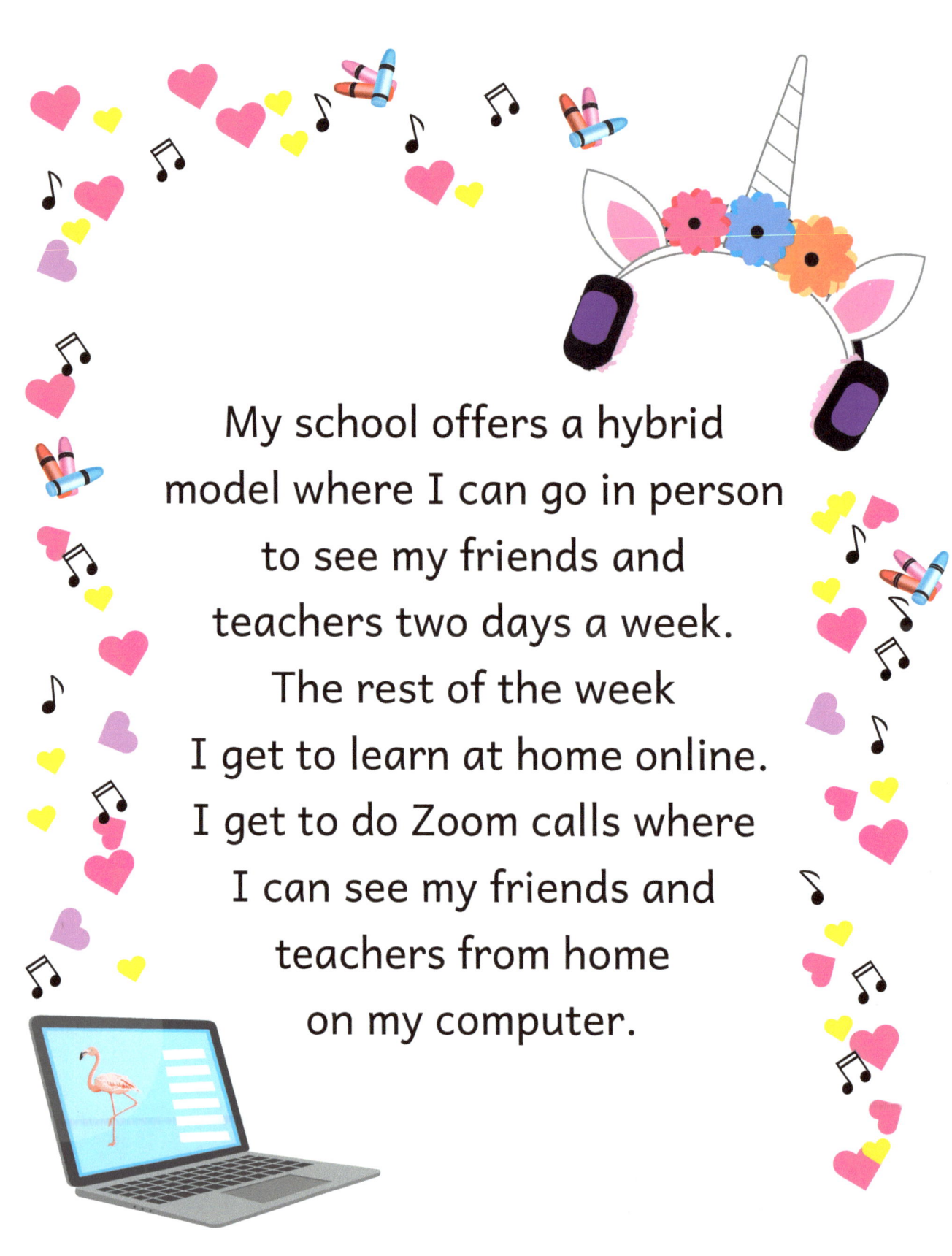

My school offers a hybrid model where I can go in person to see my friends and teachers two days a week. The rest of the week I get to learn at home online. I get to do Zoom calls where I can see my friends and teachers from home on my computer.

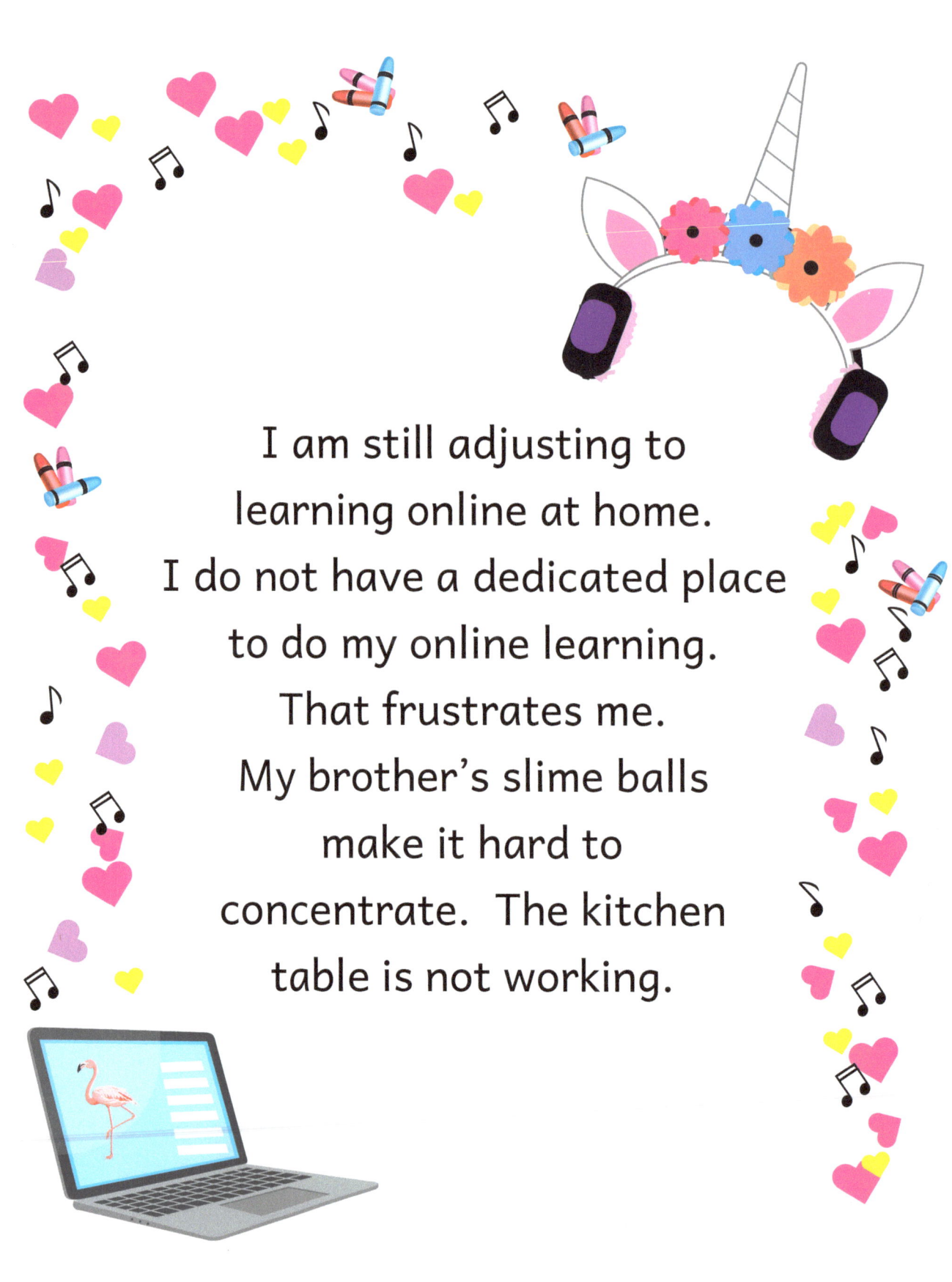

I am still adjusting to learning online at home. I do not have a dedicated place to do my online learning. That frustrates me. My brother's slime balls make it hard to concentrate. The kitchen table is not working.

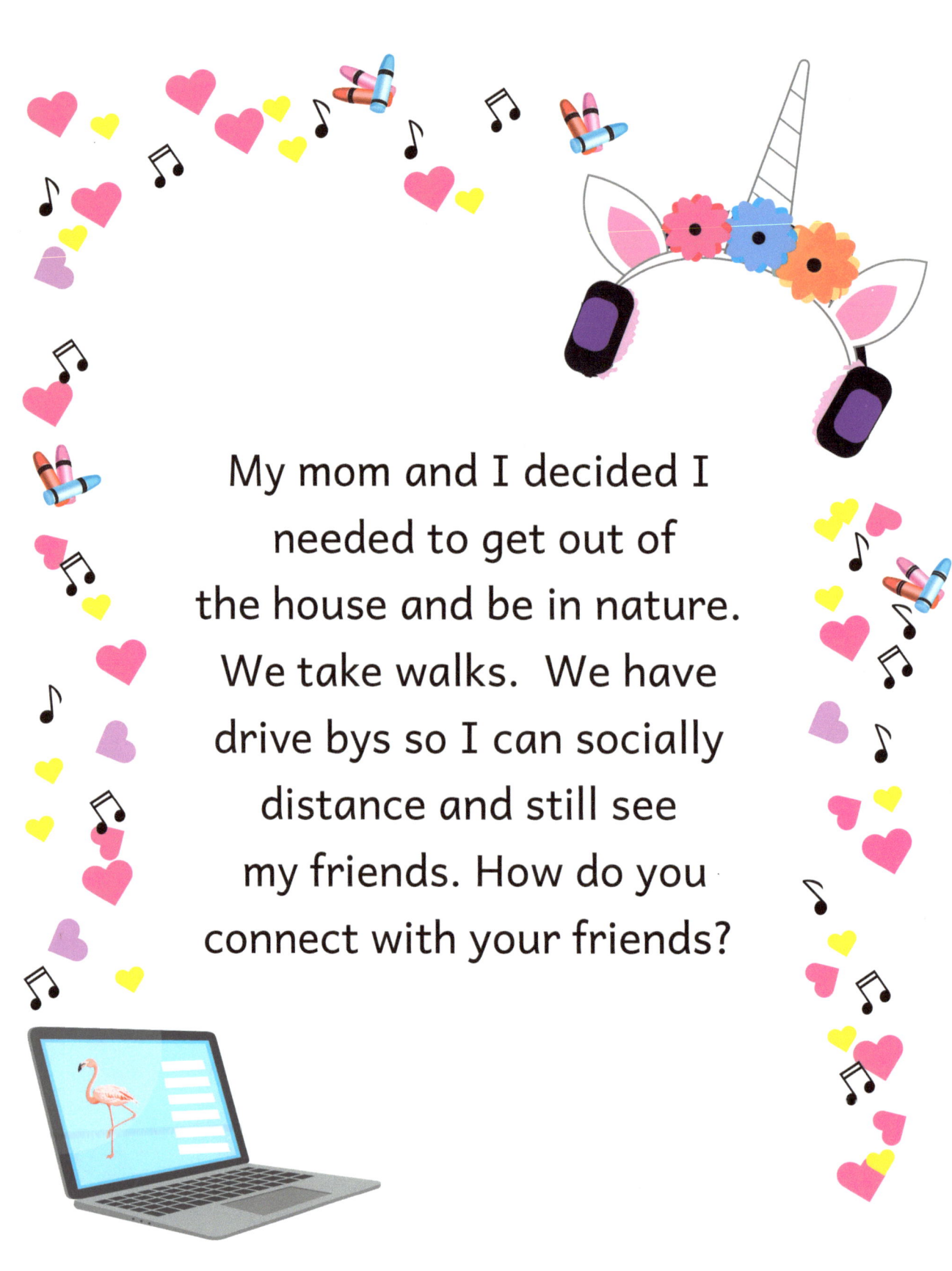

My mom and I decided I needed to get out of the house and be in nature. We take walks. We have drive bys so I can socially distance and still see my friends. How do you connect with your friends?

I realized I needed a space for home learning. I needed a desk, a lamp, a charger and a pencil box. I created my office space. My dad has an office. I feel cool like my dad!

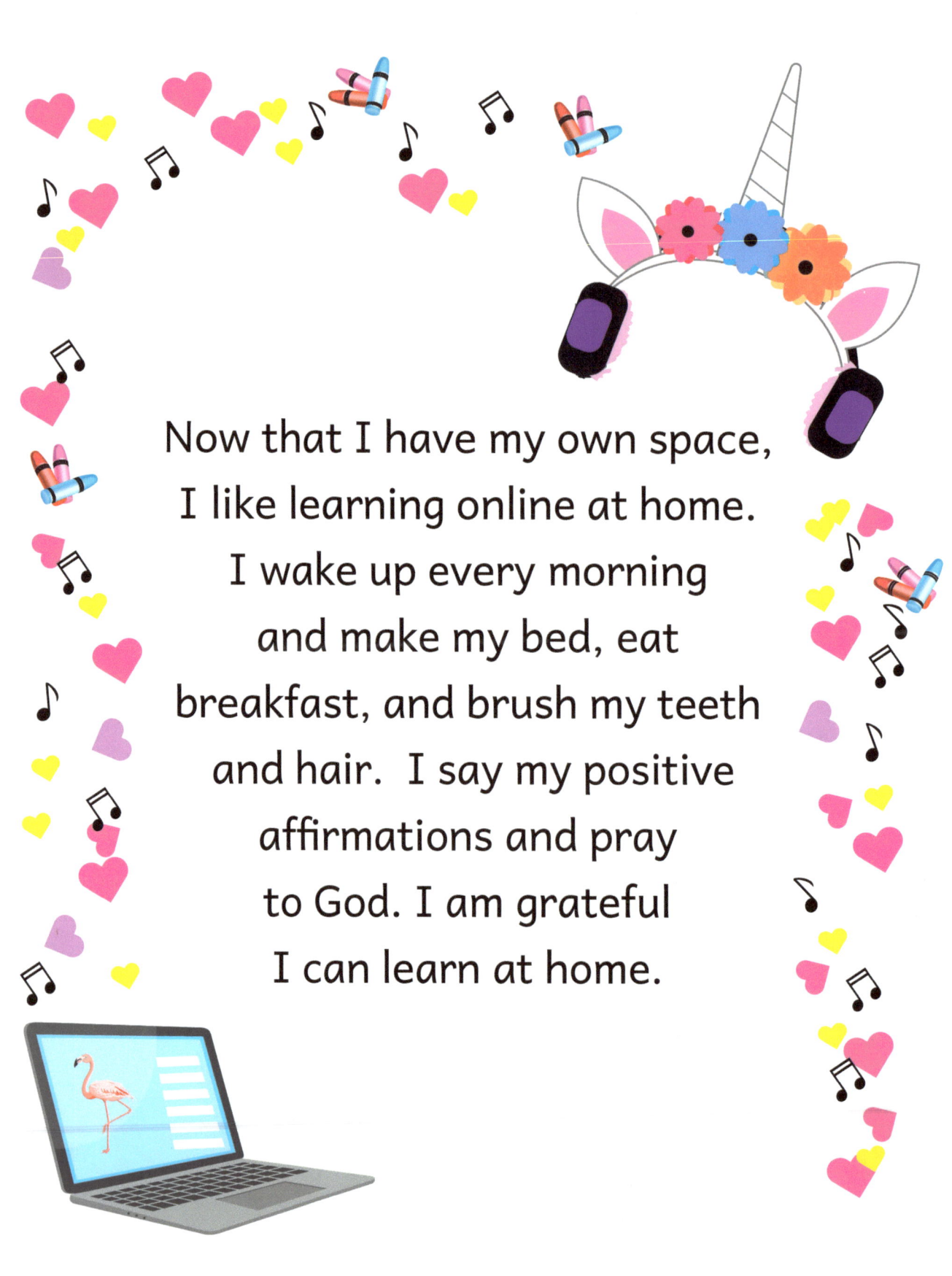

Now that I have my own space, I like learning online at home. I wake up every morning and make my bed, eat breakfast, and brush my teeth and hair. I say my positive affirmations and pray to God. I am grateful I can learn at home.

I get frustrated because sometimes the internet does not work in my home. Sometimes an app or program won't open. What makes you frustrated?

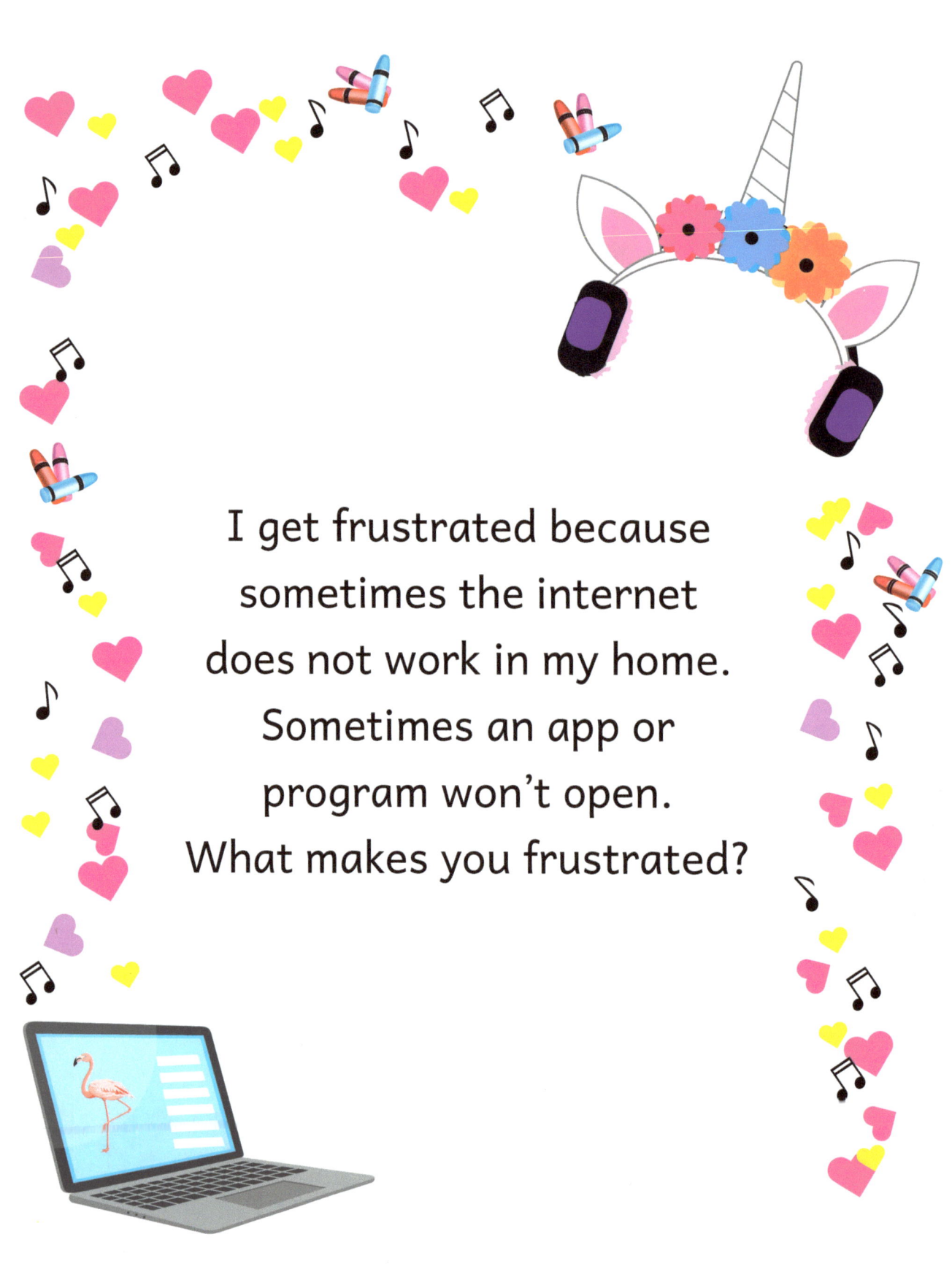

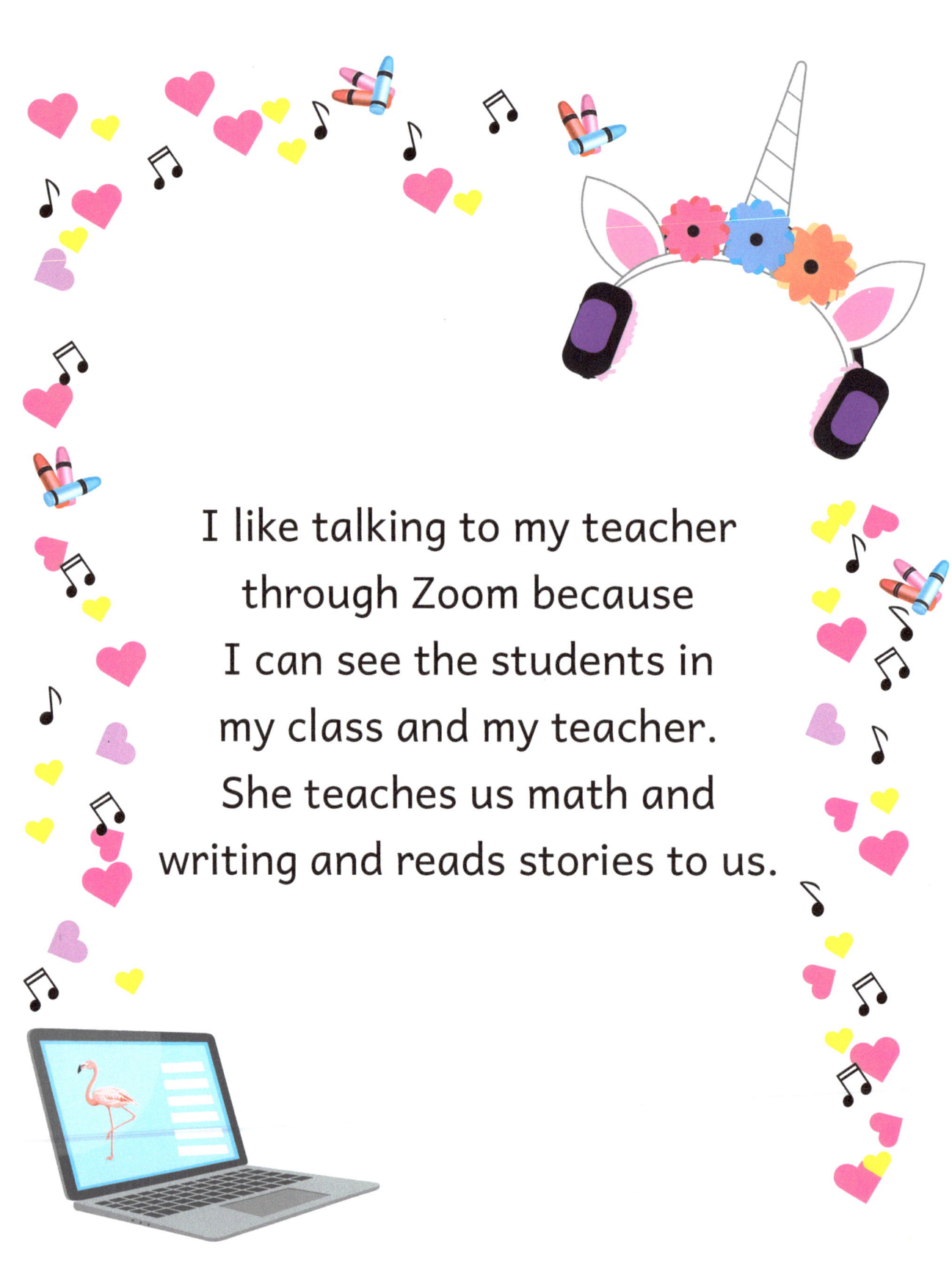

I like talking to my teacher through Zoom because I can see the students in my class and my teacher. She teaches us math and writing and reads stories to us.

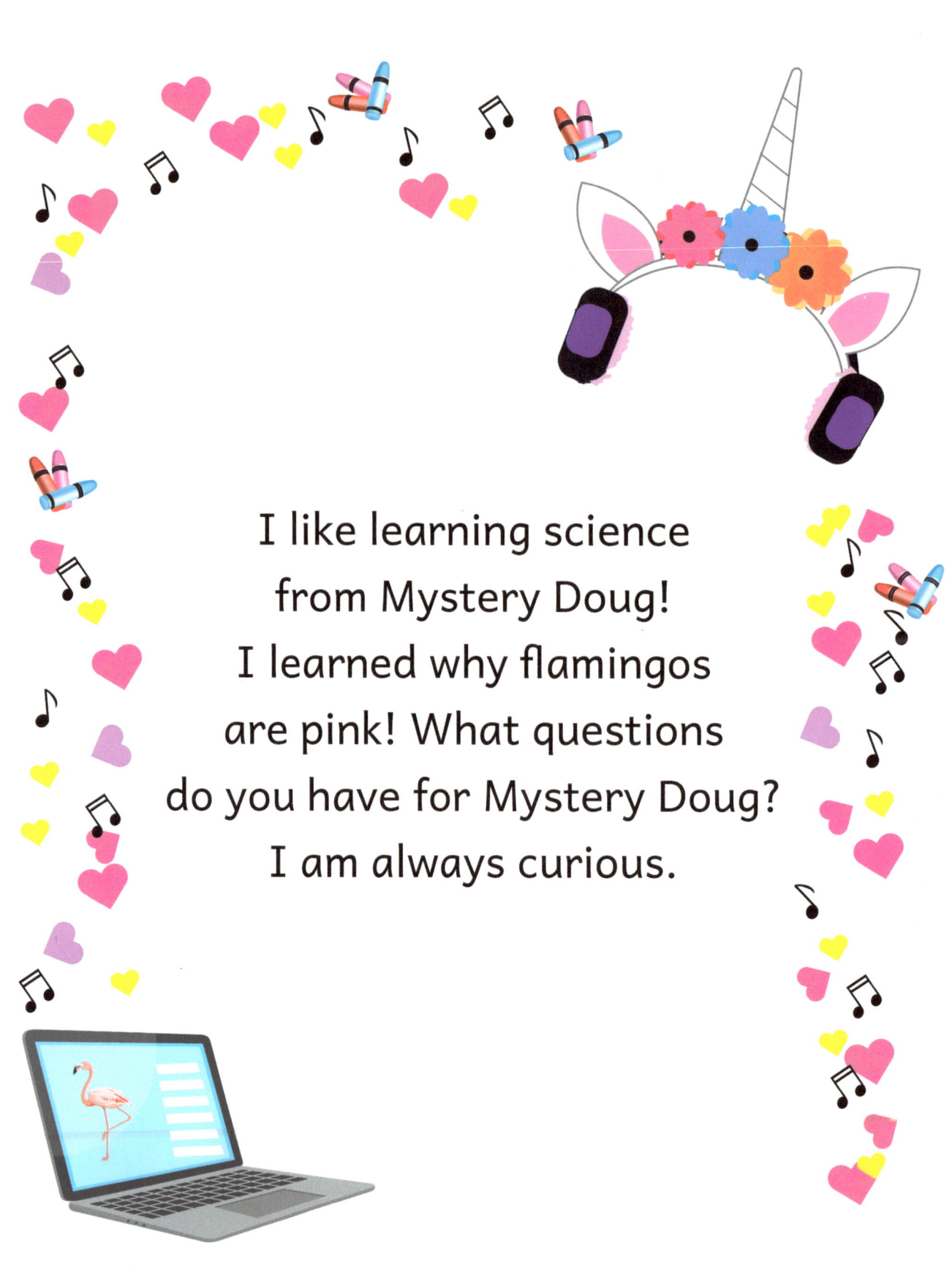

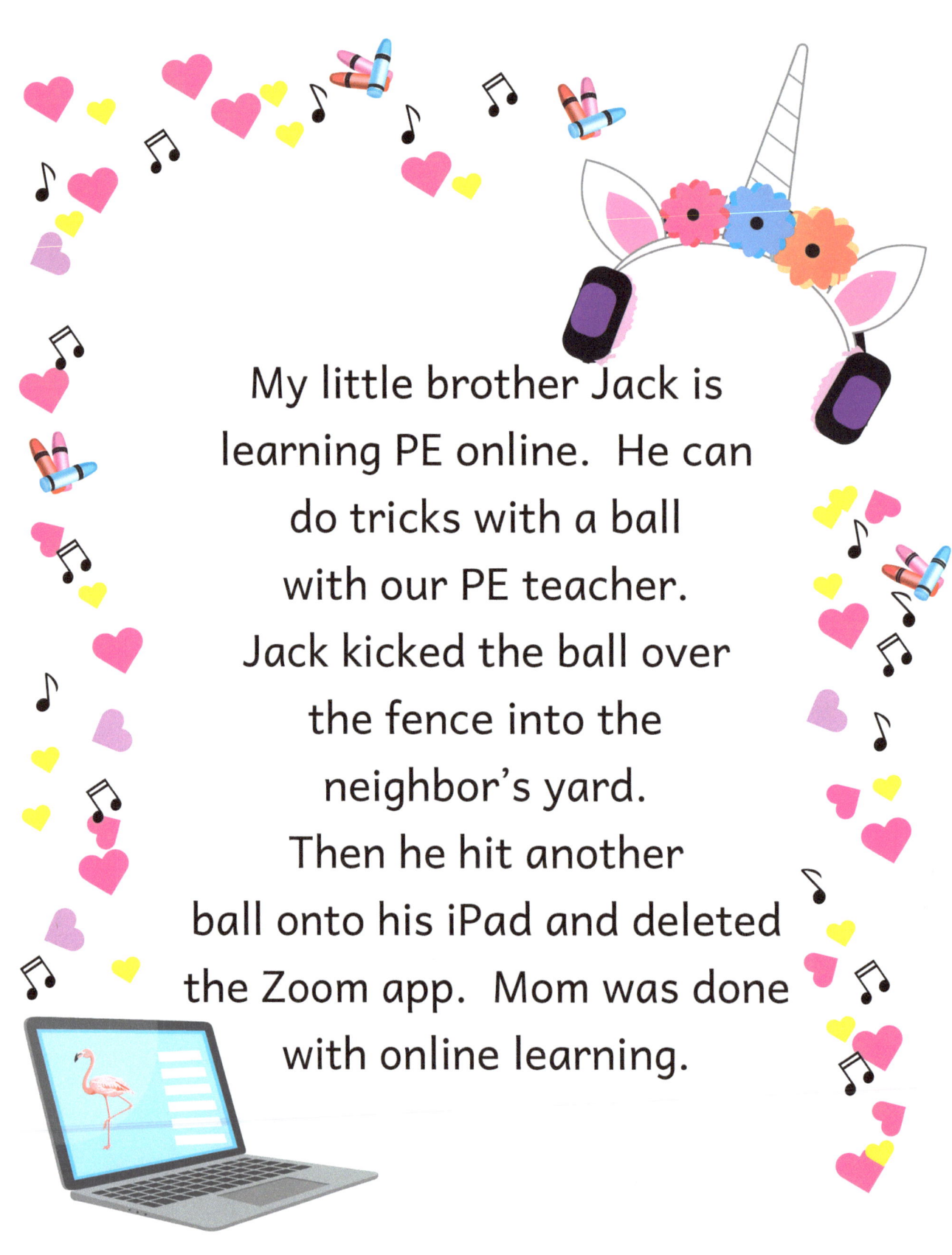

My little brother Jack is learning PE online. He can do tricks with a ball with our PE teacher. Jack kicked the ball over the fence into the neighbor's yard. Then he hit another ball onto his iPad and deleted the Zoom app. Mom was done with online learning.

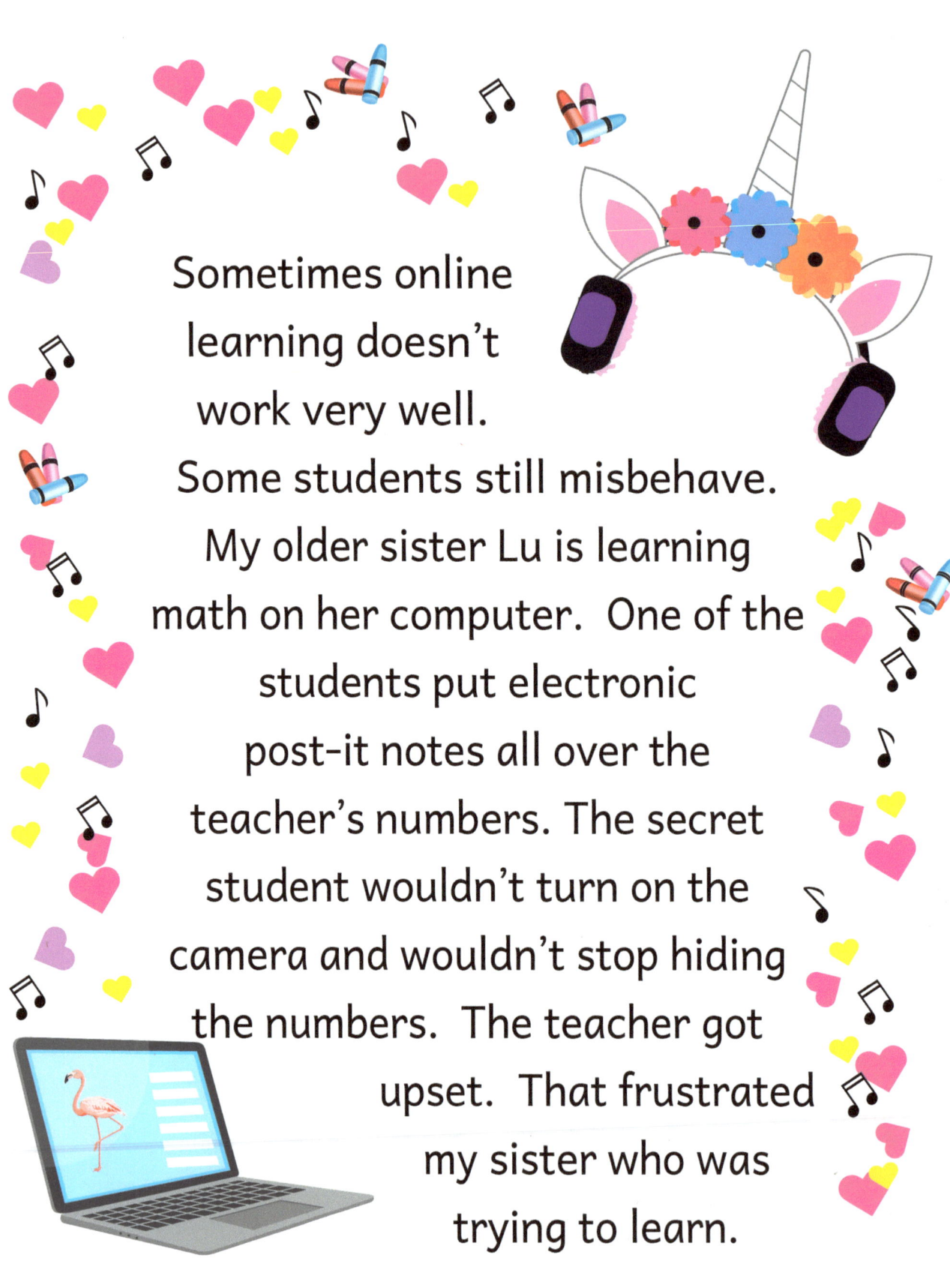

Sometimes online learning doesn't work very well. Some students still misbehave. My older sister Lu is learning math on her computer. One of the students put electronic post-it notes all over the teacher's numbers. The secret student wouldn't turn on the camera and wouldn't stop hiding the numbers. The teacher got upset. That frustrated my sister who was trying to learn.

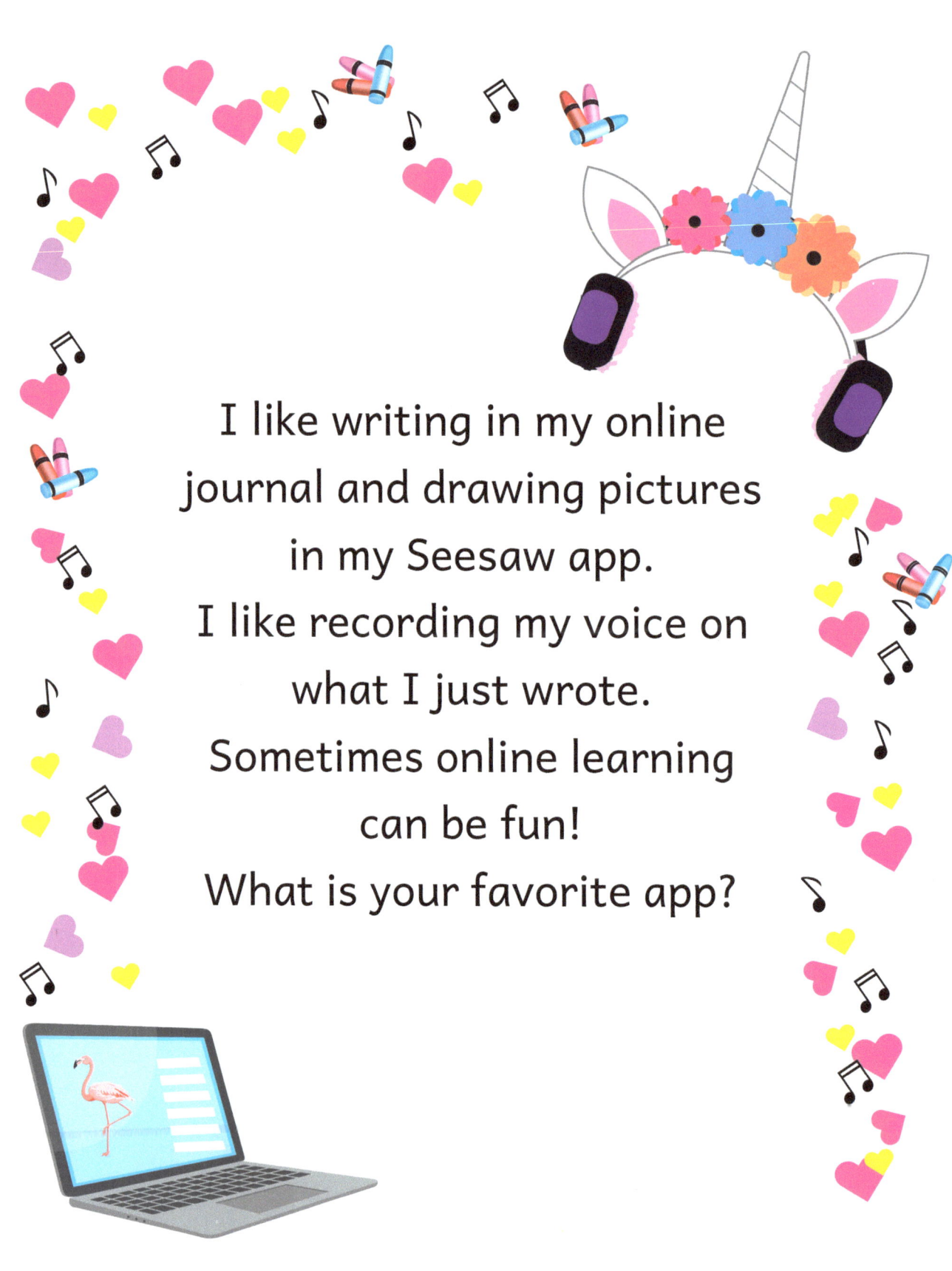

I like writing in my online journal and drawing pictures in my Seesaw app.
I like recording my voice on what I just wrote.
Sometimes online learning can be fun!
What is your favorite app?

I like to use a checklist to keep me organized. Soft, relaxing music keeps me calm. I need brain breaks so I can stay focused. What brain breaks do you enjoy most?

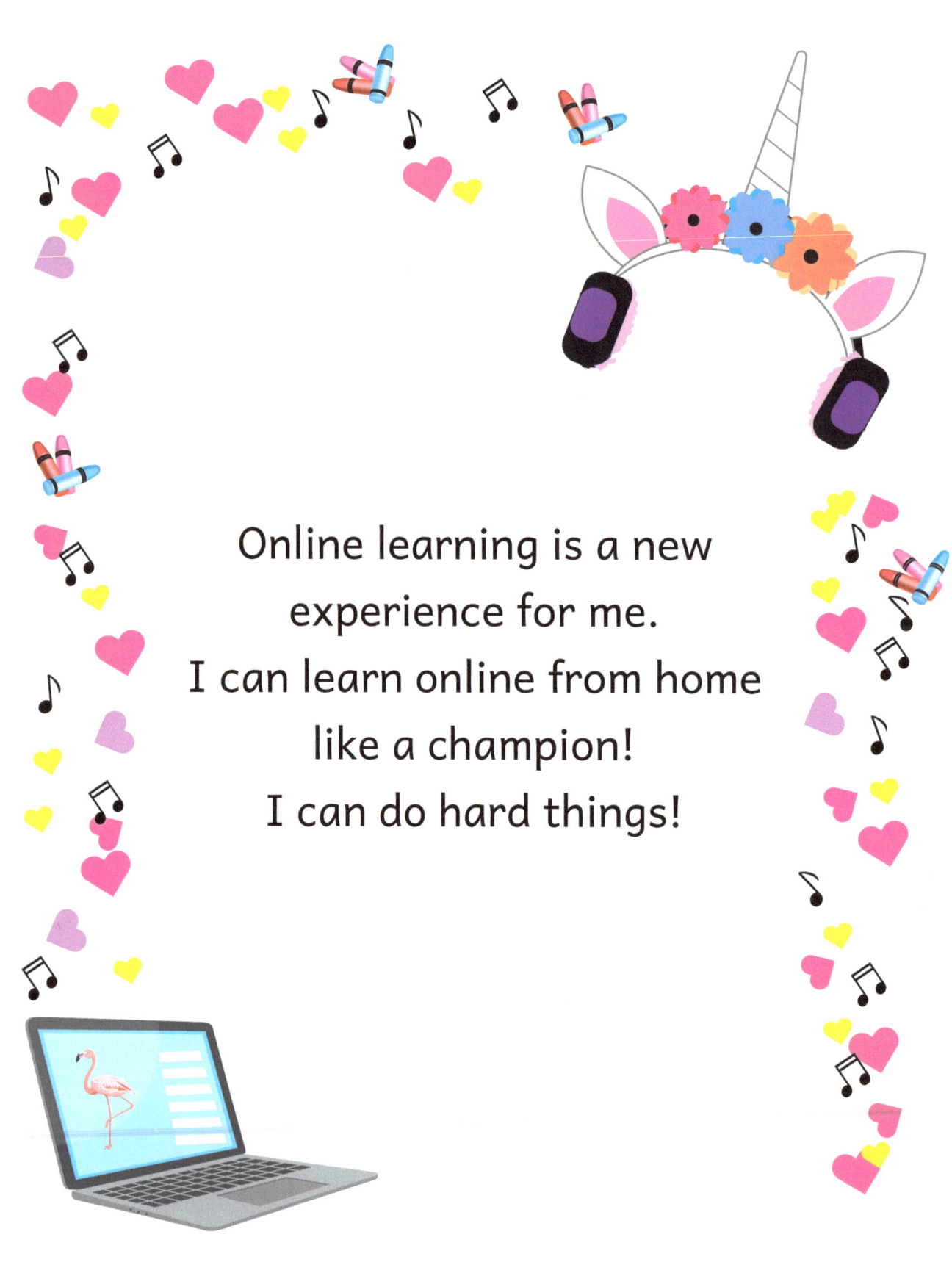

FUN FACTS

Hybrid learning
Is education involving both online or distance learning and in-person instruction.
www.wiktionary.com

Online learning
Refers to learning that is facilitated wholly by the use of digital tools and technology.
www.schoology.com

App
= application

💻 Zoey can do hard things. What hard things can you do?

💻 💻 Zoey learns about different ways to "go to school". How do you learn math, reading and writing?

💻 💻 💻 Zoey learns she needs brain breaks. What brain breaks do you do to help you stay focused?

Meet the Contributors

Aaliyah
Aaliyah is our oldest, and will be a senior next year. Online learning was definitely a struggle for classes like Chemistry and Trigonometry. She contributed to her high school poms team winning the Colorado State Championship, All American and All Colorado, and plays on the high school golf team.

Akyra
Akyra is now officially a teenager and loves hanging with her friends. Online learning was a big challenge as she really enjoys and needs a teacher guiding her. Apraxia of Speech, a motor speech disorder, has definitely affected her learning, and she embraces the challenge. Akyra enjoys playing golf with her dad and has quite the humor, making everyone laugh. She also loves HGTV.

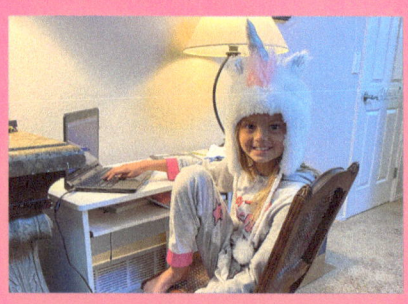

Amaya
Amaya was recently awarded the Kind Friend award, and that describes Amaya perfectly. She loves her friends and works hard. Things do not come easy or natural to Amaya, as she also has Apraxia of Speech, and daily she works hard to better understand how to overcome this disability. Amaya enjoys competitive dance, sports like basketball and golf, and riding her bike to King Soopers grocery store. Cookie dough is her favorite snack.

Akayla

Akayla struggled at first with online and hybrid learning, but gradually learned tricks to help her stay focused that are described and inspired in the book. For example, playing inspiring music, post-it notes with a "To Do" list, and taking brain breaks to help her stay focused. Apraxia of Speech has also affected her learning and development. Akayla enjoys competitive dance, playing sports like basketball and golf, and riding her bike on the trails.

CJ

Charles Jr, CJ, named in honor of his dad, loves his teachers in school. He says online learning was hard, and is grateful to be back in school full time, or at least until the next quarantine. Apraxia of Speech has also been a part of his struggles in school. CJ enjoys playing sports, like basketball, flag football, and golf.

Alyvia

Alyvia recently graduated from preschool and is excited to be a big girl in kindergarten. She says online learning was very hard as she likes the personal interaction and engagement with her teachers. She enjoys dancing, and playing with her LOL and OMG dolls.

Meet the Author

AJ Kikumoto is an up and coming female author and owner of Yellow Daisy Publishing Company. She is a super mom to 6 kids, 4 of whom have the invisible disability of Childhood Apraxia of Speech (CAS), a motor speech disorder. Her Master's degree in Elementary Education has helped her take on the challenges of guiding her children through the difficulties of Apraxia of Speech. The many hours of therapy, and different challenges with each child, proved an ever- changing learning atmosphere and mode of communication. She wanted to increase awareness and help educate the public in Apraxia of Speech.

AJ uses her expertise from dancing with the NBA Denver Nuggets Dancers and currently coaches a youth dance team, to empower the girls to follow their dreams, to believe in themselves, and to be 21st century boss babes in these unprecedented times. As a competitor for Mrs. Colorado America, her legacy project is promoting #beautyisinclusion and #youcandohardthings. Zoey's Great Adventures book series is based on the events in the lives of the author and her children. AJ teaches parents and children alike, the power of a positive mindset, anti-bullying, and good societal morals and values.

www.ingramcontent.com/pod-product-compliance
Lightning Source LLC
Chambersburg PA
CBHW040758240426
43673CB00014B/388